The Realm Of God

Unlocking the Supernatural

DR. TEMISAN SMART

CHAPTERS

DEDICATION

First of all, I thank God for His faithfulness and mercy over my life.
thank my — ever-so-beautiful wife — for her tireless support;
you are indeed a true help-meet to me. To my beautiful children,
Misan and Timeyin, you are the best kids in the whole world.

To my church family, Kingdom Life Ministry Global, I am super
proud to be your pastor.
To all those who desire a deeper walk with God, as you read this
book, may you have visitations and life-changing encounters in
Jesus' name. Amen.

FORWARD

I have known Dr. Temi Smart for 13 years and have developed a deep love and respect for our friendship. I found in his writing this book for the Christian Community, Dr. Smart has put together a captivating and inspirational piece of work.

My prayer is, as you who dare to read this magnificent work written by my friend, Dr. Temi Smart; you would increase in the authority and power given to us by God through the death and resurrection of his Son, Jesus Christ. Thank you, Dr. Smart, for sharing this divine revelation with the body of Christ; and given me years of your friendship. Blessing and peace be upon all as you embark upon living from your Spirit man!

Bishop Arthur Felton Jr.
Senior pastor, World Changers Worship Center, Greenville Texas

I am so thrilled that a much needed and timely book is now in our hands and available to readers worldwide. Dr. Temi Smart's "The Realm of God" takes us on a profound journey into the supernatural realm with God, inviting us into a dimension of deep revelation like never before. This book is a must-read because it guides us on a deep journey of intimacy with God, instilling a profound Godly discipline in how we approach the divine realm and understand our purpose here on Earth.

I am honored for this timely revelation that points us to God through the insightful and inspired work of Dr. Temi Smart.

Dr. Mike Kingsley
President and Founder, World Trumpet TV

The Realm of God!
Principles, perspectives and promises that will empower you to live beyond your wildest imagination!

It's with great joy that I read and absorbed this book entitled the Realm of God written by my good friend and fellow Minister Dr. Temisan Smart. I refer to Dr. Smart as the humble man, of the great God.

I enjoyed and devoured this simple, yet very powerful treatise which teaches and demonstrates how one can walk in the fullness of the power of God.

My favorite part of the book is when Dr. Smart said, "In the real sense, (after salvation, our supernatural spirit was born again) thus we are supernatural beings housed in a natural vessel, called the human body."

As you read, and most importantly apply by faith. these principles that Dr Smart has skillfully unveiled, you will find the similar results in your life. You will no longer crawl on the ground, but rather fly through the sky! So in essence your time as a spiritual caterpillar has expired, your wings are now ready! Read and apply this book so you can fly as God designed you to do... no more living by limiting beliefs, but rather limitless success for the glory of God and for the good of yourself and His people.

Dr. Stan Harris aka Dr. Breakthrough

This book is truly inspiring, and it's filled with real-life stories that show just how powerful the truths in these pages are—they go far beyond mere theory. What really stood out to me was the chapter on accessing the realm of God through obedience. Dr Smart, your insights in this book reflect the very essence of your life. As I read, I couldn't help but think of how your actions and faithfulness perfectly embody the lessons shared in each chapter. You don't just speak of these truths—you live them every day, showing us all what it truly means to walk in the realm of God.
Dear readers, as you prayerfully dive into this book, I pray that you too are inspired to enter the realm of God and live the life He has always intended for you.

Dr. Imaobong Smart
President, Purpose House Foundation & Seven Mountains Production.

The book (The Realm of God) is a powerful insight and

a revelational material that is most needed in this present world where gross darkness has covered the earth, we live in a world full of evil. These are the last days, and the church need to be aware of their identity to enable her to confront the manipulation of the devil.
In this book Dr Smart emphasizes how the church can understand her authority in the word of God and operate on her full personality in Christ Jesus on earth.
I recommend it to all believers and ministers who want to fully maximize their Godly nature and walk in the supernatural.

Apostle Dr. Vincent A.O Strong.
Founder: Prevailing Faith Global Ministries

INTRODUCTION

Man was originally created to live supernaturally in the natural realm. That means the natural realm was supposed to be foreign to man; however, when man fell, what we call the natural became our reality. This downgrade to our existence is simply why men keep looking for something more. Meeting God and reconciling with Him through the finished work of Jesus on the cross is returning man to that original state of supernatural manifestations. People try to find that missing link through various unauthorized means like the occultic, psychics, mediums witchcraft, and various kinds of spiritism. However, we know the only valid way to tap into the supernatural without soul-damming consequences is through a relationship with Jesus Christ.

The Bible says in
Matthew 6:9-10, *After this manner therefore pray ye: Our Father which art in heaven, Hallowed be thy name. Thy kingdom come. Thy will be done in earth, as it is in heaven.*

That prayer implies that we, as Christians, cannot operate in the natural realm to achieve the supernatural manifestation of God. Hence, Jesus taught His disciples to pray that "thy kingdom come." So, when we talk about God's kingdom coming, we refer to God's government being established in the natural. In essence, we refer to the lifestyle in God's kingdom being established on earth. Therefore, those who call upon God should live in the supernatural realm while in the natural world.

John 17:16 (KJV)
They are not of the world, even as I am not of the world.

When we talk about the Kingdom of God, we refer to the operations and culture obtained in the kingdom of heaven.

There is a limitation if we choose to live in the natural realm. So, for us to see the supernatural, we must go higher. The Bible says, "my thoughts are higher than your thoughts; my ways are higher than your ways.' So, you must come to a higher level of thought. You must come into the higher realm, where God lives.

Isaiah 55:8-9 *"For my thoughts are not your thoughts, neither are your ways my ways," declares the LORD. "As the heavens are higher than the earth, so are my ways higher than your ways and my thoughts than your thoughts."*

I am here to establish how to live and walk in the realm where all things are possible. In the natural, things may appear impossible, but in the realm of God, all things are possible. In the book of John chapter 11:20-25, when Lazarus died, to the natural man, it was impossible for Lazarus to see life again. However, our Master who operated in the supernatural realm said, "Lazarus shall live again." Martha and Mary explained, "We know that he will live; maybe someday when the world has come to an end, he will come back and live again.' However, Jesus said, "No, I'm saying, that he will live again because in the realm where I operate from, all things are possible."

My goal in writing this book is to stir up a desire in you to come up higher to where God lives so that you can show this dying world that our faith in Jesus is not a farce and that everything, we claim to believe in the Bible is a reality.

One slogan that describes everything I do is "SHORT, SHARP AND LOADED."

Many people will assume that writing about the realm of God has to be 5000 pages long, but no…it doesn't have to be; God enjoys simplicity. Besides, if you need a 5000-page book to transform you, you probably have no desire to be transformed.

I desire for everyone to pick up this book, have wakeup moments and encounters as they read and finish this book, pray the simple but heartfelt prayers attached to each chapter, and be transformed.

CHAPTER 1
WHERE GOD LIVES

When we talk about the realm of God, it simply means the lifestyle of God, His culture, His atmosphere, aura, and the possibilities available in His environment. It means the operations of God and the principles that govern the kingdom of God.

The Bible says in the book of Isaiah 55:8,
"For my thoughts are not your thoughts, neither are your ways my ways. For as the heavens are higher than the earth, so are my ways higher than your ways, and my thoughts than your thoughts."

So, it means that how God thinks and how we think are completely different. God's perspective is superior to ours; it means that there is something in the realm where God lives that is different from the one we live in.

The things that happen in the realm where God lives are called supernatural because they are superior to whatever happens here in our natural world. This realm where we live (Earth or physical realm) is governed by the five senses and is limited in every way possible.

Many may assume that anything that cannot be logically explained within the five senses is nonexistent and that all the possibilities available to us are only in this realm. However, I beg to differ: all human beings, no matter the disposition you currently hold on to, are made in God's image and likeness. Although some of our realities have been veiled and hidden as a result of the fall we experienced in Genesis, nevertheless, man are still aware of the supernatural dimensions, and the proof is in man's desires to tap into places that seem unreachable, desires to astro project, travel faster, read minds, etc. Even in our movies, almost every story delves more into the spiritual side of life. Truth is, there is a missing piece to our full identity. There are two keys that can open up the portal into the supernatural: the keys provided by God through a sincere relationship with Him via the word and prayer, and the keys provided by demonic influences. God desires for us to walk in the supernatural realm because so many earthly realities are dependent on the supernatural for their manifestation.

John 10:34, *"Is it not written in your law I say ye are gods."*

For some overly religious folks, this scripture may seem like heresy to quote and believe in, not because it is blasphemy but because of the mindset that has been robbed of the truth of our true identity in God. It is more ignorant than humble to deny the truth of this verse, and try to explain it away. No wonder Jesus wept over Jerusalem because of their ignorance. God did not create us to be ordinary, and His intention for us concerning our supernatural identity is spread all over the Bible, from Genesis to Revelation. For example, Elijah outrunning a chariot on foot is not a natural phenomenon. The three Hebrew boys thrown into the fire but not consumed by it are definitely not natural. What about Philip teleporting from one place to another, or even Peter telling the lame to walk? Everyone who truly walked with God lived or had encounters beyond the possibilities of the earthly realm. They were able to tap into a more superior realm — the realm where God lives.

So, brace yourself for an exposition and be prepared to unlearn and relearn. If the word of God rightly divided by the Holy Spirit is the basis for your judgment and conclusions, then I encourage you to open up your heart and let the veil hiding your true identity and possibilities be ripped off your face.

It has been God's desire from the beginning of time to bring us into the realm where we can manifest the fullness of Himself in us. When we understand the importance of jurisdiction in where we operate, then our status as gods will no longer be a strange phenomenon to us. Being gods implies that we express a part of us that is more supernatural than natural because, in the real sense, we are supernatural beings housed in a natural vessel called the human body.

It is quite unfortunate that most people can only grasp

this concept when it has to do with demonic possession, we see and hear of how a person hosting a demonic entity in their body can do superhuman things. For example, the mad man at Gadara would break strong chains used to hold him bound and overpower many strong men. Also, remember the seven sons of Sceva; they were beaten and overcome by one man who was demon-possessed. When we hear stories like this, it does not amaze us because that is what we expect to see when a spirit from another realm takes over a human's body. I mean, I have heard of a little girl who was demon-possessed, picking up a grown man like a doll and even levitating. Why is this not strange to man? It baffles me that when a Christian who houses the Holy Spirit does anything out of the ordinary, we are quick to say its fake or it is demon-influenced. How come Satan inhabiting a body can do supernatural things, but God inhabiting a body can't? Do you see how Satan has managed to make many believe that he is the only one with supernatural possibilities, that as a child of God, you should not dream or dare to manifest your supernatural dimension?

Would you agree with me that you are gods on earth? Please note that I am not referring to us as equals to our God almighty. This is why I refer to us as "gods" in lower cases.

In Genesis, God said let them have dominion over the earth. Dominion implies rulership over all things; it means that the earth and its circumstances are subject to us and must obey us. We see examples of Moses parting the Red Sea, Joshua commanding the sun to stand still, and Jesus commanding the winds to be still. Let me share with you a testimony that happened in our church, Kingdom Life Ministry Global. We had a young girl who was pregnant, and her baby had been monitored and diagnosed by two specialists that he would come out with Down syndrome and his legs would be abnormally short. The young girl was distraughted, to say the least. The mother brought her to church, and we prayed specific prayers over the baby; we commanded the baby to be normal head to toe, that same week, the baby was born perfect and healthy, and now he is running around and enjoying every minute of his precious life!

We are not gods in the sense that demands worship; when it comes to worship, only God almighty, the maker of all things, is deserving and worthy of worship.

So, take off the hat of what you already know and let us journey into the realm of God that we, as heirs, should partake in unashamedly.

WORKBOOK

1. What does the realm of God mean to you?

2. How does the Bible describe God's thoughts and ways in Isaiah 55:8?

3. What are the two keys that can open up the portal into the supernatural?

4. Share a personal experience or testimony of supernatural encounter or manifestation.

5. What changes do you need to make to start walking in your supernatural identity?

CHAPTER 2

THE REALM OF GOD—LOVE

John 14:21 says: *"He that hath my commandments, and keep them, he it is that loves me: and he that loveth me shall be loved of my Father, and I will love him, and will manifest myself to him."*

If we want to see God manifest Himself in our world today, we must love Him. Only those who love God will see His kingdom come.

God requires from us a love that is so intense and completely surrendered.

Luke 14:26-27:
If any man come to me, and hate not his father, and mother, and wife, and children, and brethren, and sisters, yea, and his own life also, he cannot be my disciple. And whosoever doth not bear his cross, and come after me, cannot be my disciple.

You can love your family as you should, but do not let it compare to the love you have for God.

God is saying, "Where I want to be in your life, no one should be elevated to that place."

Meaning that He will not share His position in your life, nor will He alternate with your next best thing. The kind of love that will command the supernatural is the kind of love that will make people question your sanity. That is the kind of love God is expecting from us all — the highest, most intense affection humanly possible.

Many Christians of today want to command the supernatural, but they have a lot of things that compete with their love for God, and those other things are winning most of the time. Our businesses are winning; our addictions, our children, and many other distractions are winning. God is saying, "I can't manifest myself when I can't confidently say I'm your top-most priority."

God's jealousy is more than what men have for their wives; I know most of you can think of a scenario where you felt jealous because your partner seemed to have put something or someone above you (pause and reminisce the emotions you exuded at that moment).

THE PROOF OF YOUR LOVE
1. You must prioritize God and His services

In loving God, you must prioritize God and His services above everything else. It does not matter what that thing is; God must never take the rear seat of your life. This is how to test your priority level towards a thing or person. When you find out that no matter how tired or stressed out you are, you find yourself giving sacrificial attention to a thing or person, then that person or thing has a high priority in your life. For example, some people have put God and His services as the lowest priority. In the sense that, no matter how tired they are, they still get up and drag themselves to work Monday through Friday and would probably volunteer to drag themselves on Saturday morning if they are requested to come in, all for the money. Unfortunately, these same people, even in the best conditions, are hardly able to find time to pray, read their Bible, talk less of driving to church. The same circumstance that was weak in power to keep them from their job or hanging out with friends was powerful enough to keep them from attending a church service, going out to evangelize, or even spending time in prayers.

It's unfortunate that when it comes to the services of God, He always gets the crumbs that we, flawed as we are, would reject. At this point, I will give you an opportunity to check yourself. Why does this tiredness that could not keep you from work keep you from attending to the father's business? Where your treasure is, there your heart would be. What you love is what you do crazy sacrificial acts for.

Are you prioritizing other things/people above God?

2. You must make sacrifices for someone you love

Let's get out of this crazy new message that is going around that whatever you do for God must always be at your convenience. Let's look at a scenario: How many of you have gone into a relationship, and every time you plan a date, something always comes up, and the other person says something like, "Sorry I have to cancel, it's not convenient, I can't make the date." You might be polite enough to understand the first time but how will you react after two or more cancellations? You'd probably wonder, "Can't this person just make a sacrifice once?" A young man who was in love with a lady said to her, "I will cross the seven seas and climb the highest mountain for you." One day, they had planned to meet up when it started to rain, then he called her and said, "I'm sorry, I can't see you today because it's raining." So, he would cross the seven seas but couldn't withstand a little rain?

You can laugh it out! That's the level of some people. What they say is different from what they do. The sacrifices that you are ready to make for the sake of the kingdom is an indication of how much you love God. We do not serve a God who only tells us what to do, our God went all out and showed us what PERFECT sacrifice looks like when He gave something He loved so much. He sacrificed Jesus! A wise king in the Bible called David, knew the mystery of sacrifice that unlocks the supernatural; that's why He said, "I will not give God what cost me nothing, if your acts of service or your giving does not touch you or hurt your heart then it was an act of convenience NOT an act of sacrifice.

Your sacrifice includes your time; your sleep, your TV time, etc., on a daily basis. It also includes your finances and everything you hold dear.

That's how you make sacrifices. A heart madly in love with God and desperate to prove that love would say things like this, "God, your word says I should bring my 10%. It's not convenient for me, but because I love you, and I love your work, I'm bringing my 10%." "God, I know it's not convenient for me to go to church today because I am tired, but because I love you and your word. I am breaking every protocol; I am carrying myself there." That is sacrifice.

3. You talk about Him everywhere you go
I am that husband who finds a way to talk about my wife wherever I go because I love her and am proud of who she is. One of my spiritual daughters went out with her friend's fiancée for a business meeting. Let's call her friend Sally; after the meeting, Sally called and started asking, "Did my fiancée talk about me? Did he tell people he was engaged?' etc. What does that have to do with anything? She wanted to know how proud he was of her. You can't love God and be silent about Him. It is not possible. I sing out some gospel songs whenever I am in a store because, somehow, I want an opportunity to talk about Jesus. You can laugh, but that has always been one of my strategies, and it has worked over the years.

4. You must spend time with Him
Whether in church, in His word, or in prayers. Many people attend church only to end up looking at the time and wonder when they will share the grace. They do not find joy or pleasure in being in the congregation of His people. Any time you come to church, no matter how close or familiar you are with everyone, carry in you the awareness that you didn't come to meet man; you came to meet God. The time you pray, attend church, and read your Bible is all precious time with Him. When you tarry in His presence, you know His moves, you become more acquainted with His voice.

You no longer say things like "something told me." You will boldly say "God told me."

5. You Don't Hold on To Offenses

When You Love Someone: Some people are not in church anymore and even left the faith because they were angry with God. They felt God did not answer all their prayers, thus letting them down. They hold on to "offenses." When they come to church, they are careful to note every little thing that displeases them and are quick to walk away. When God revealed to me that my mom was going to die, I prayed against it with all my heart. One day, I called her, took an anointing oil, called my siblings, and prayed some more.

She eventually died after everything! I was very angry, and I questioned God. "Why did you reveal to me my mom's death if you did not plan to keep her alive.?" I was thinking, crying, and saying different things. But I still left room for God's sovereignty; I remember saying something to this effect. "God, you know this was going to happen, and you allowed it to happen. I acknowledge you know better than me; I surrender to your will." And I said, "God, take the glory; I find no fault in you." It was tough to accept what had happened to my mother, but who was I to be offended by my loving father?

1 Peter 4:8. *"Above all things, have fervent charity among yourselves, for charity shall cover multitude of sins."*

Whenever you feel offended, swiftly let go because your love for God supersedes all offenses.

6. Loyalty is the ability to stay put with a thing or a person irrespective of the odds.

It is an unmovable allegiance towards a cause or a person.

1 Corinthians 4:2, *"It is required of stewards that they be found faithful." NIV*

Proverbs 20:6, "Most men will proclaim everyone his own goodness: but a faithful man who can find?"
I would like to start by saying that loyalty is not a word to put you under bondage or subjection to anyone; it is not received, but it is shared. Do you know that God is so loyal to you? Yes, He is. The Bible says that "while we were yet sinners Christ died for us." When we despised, hated, and just didn't care about Him, He was still devoted to loving us. Pause for a moment and just thank God for His faithful love towards you.

Loyalty does not care for convenience.

John 6:66-68, *"At this point many of his disciples turned away and deserted him. Then Jesus turned to the Twelve and asked, "Are you also going to leave?"*
Simon Peter replied, "Lord, to whom would we go? You have the words that give eternal life."

This was a very tough situation where the 12 had to back the crowd. Jesus had just preached a message that was hard to digest, and people took offense. Many deserted him, but those who were truly loyal stuck with Him. One of the missing ingredients in relationships today is loyalty. Most people simply want to hang around where the sun is shining, but as soon as the clouds get grey, they move to the next sunny side. Such people never truly grow or build meaningful relationships with a place or a people. When you love somebody, you give them your allegiance. You don't serve God only when the going is good. You don't stand on the fence with a plan to jump to the other side if things don't go the way you want. Another example of true loyalty was between David and his friend Jonathan.

Jonathan was so loyal to his friend David even at the cost of his father's throne. This, for me, is one of the most powerful illustrations of loyalty. It is easy to appear loyal when you have nothing to lose, but when you have to choose between loyalty to things and loyalty to God, that is when you know where you truly stand. The young and rich ruler in the book of Mark 10 thought he was loyal to the laws of God until he had to choose.

Mark 10:17-27 (KJV)
And when he was gone forth into the way, there came one running, and kneeled to him, and asked him, Good Master, what shall I do that I may inherit eternal life? And Jesus said unto him, Why callest thou me good? there is none good but one, that is, God. Thou knowest the commandments, Do not commit adultery, Do not kill, Do not steal, Do not bear false witness, Defraud not, Honour thy father and mother. And he answered and said unto him, Master, all these have I observed from my youth. Then Jesus beholding him loved him, and said unto him, One thing thou lackest: go thy way,

sell whatsoever thou hast, and give to the poor, and thou shalt have treasure in heaven: and come, take up the cross, and follow me. And he was sad at that saying, and went away grieved: for he had great possessions. And Jesus looked round about, and saith unto his disciples, How hardly shall they that have riches enter into the kingdom of God! And the disciples were astonished at his words. But Jesus answereth again, and saith unto them, Children, how hard is it for them that trust in riches to enter into the kingdom of God! It is easier for a camel to go through the eye of a needle, than for a rich man to enter into the kingdom of God. And they were astonished out of measure, saying among themselves, Who then can be saved? And Jesus looking upon them saith, With men it is impossible, but not with God: for with God all things are possible.

In conclusion, if you must walk in the realm of God, you must love him with all your heart, with all your might and with all your strength- Mark 12:30-31.

Everything God does is powered by Love and before he manifest himself through a man, he vets their heart to see if they love him above everything else. Are you ready to Love God more than you do right now?

Let Us Pray
Lord, help me to love you beyond the letters. Help me to love you more than anything I hold dear. I declare that I love you and pledge my allegiance to you.
I pray that my heart will be connected to you. That you will manifest yourself in every facet of my life.

In the name of Jesus. Amen.

WORKBOOK

1. What does John 14:21 say about loving God and keeping His commandments?

2. How can you prioritize God and His services in your daily life?

3. What are some areas where you can make sacrifices for God?

4. How can you remain loyal to God despite challenges or difficulties?

5. What changes do you need to make to deepen your love for God?

CHAPTER 3
THE REALM OF
GOD — OBEDIENCE

What is obedience?
Obedience is an act of promptly doing exactly what one has been instructed to do, whether it makes sense or not.

KINDS OF OBEDIENCE
1. Willful and complete obedience
Like Abraham's actions when he was told to sacrifice his son, Isaac. He did not negotiate or grumble; he went out in complete obedience to honor what God had commanded him to do.

Genesis 17:22-23 *"When he had finished speaking with Abraham, God went up from him. On that very day Abraham took his son Ishmael and all those born in his household or bought with his money, every male in his household, and circumcised them, as God told him."*

Another example of this kind of obedience is when the servant at the wedding ceremony in Cannan—followed to the T—the instruction of Jesus to present the wedding guest with a jar of water which later turned into the best wine they ever had. John chapter 2 from verse one to the end.

2. Delayed/grumbled Obedience

Delayed obedience is when one obeys but not at the right time. Usually, delayed obedience is inspired when grumbling is in play. Grumbling is when one obeys God with an attitude of complaining and murmuring. An example of this is when prophet Elisha told Naaman to wash himself in the Jordan River. He almost missed his healing because he didn't like the instructions, but thanks be to GOD for his right-hand man who persuaded him to obedience.

There was a time we instructed our daughter to do the dishes before we returned home from our outing. She spent the whole time playing, and as soon as she heard the car pull in the driveway, she ran to the kitchen and began to do the dishes. My wife and I were upset about her disobedience, she explained that she did not disobey us as she was currently doing the dishes, but this was disobedience because the instruction we gave her wasn't carried out at the time that we instructed. Delayed obedience is literally no obedience at all. When God asks you to do something, how promptly do you carry out what God instructs, many times, delayed obedience makes people miss out on a NOW blessing.

When God asks some people to do something, they want to consult with Mr. A, and Mrs. B to ask all the relevant and irrelevant questions about the instruction. By the time they are done with their investigations, the desired time to carry out the act of obedience passes. This doesn't go down well with God. Let's look at

Psalms 119:60. It says: *"I made haste and delayed not to keep thy commandments."*

Abraham obeyed God when he said, "Go and sacrifice Isaac." He did not even wait for Sarah, his wife, to wake up; he carried the child off. Be rest assured that although God loves you, you are dispensable. Meaning that when God gives an urgent instruction about something very important, when you delay or disobey, God will raise another to take your place and do His bidding. Before you know it, the blessing that was to come to you by reason of that obedience goes to another person. Delayed obedience is disobedience. How many of you will ask your child to do something at a certain time, and they say, "I will do it when I want," and you will be okay with that? You want them to do it when you want them to do it, right? That's the logic.

Don't discuss God's instructions with people who struggle with obeying instructions.

In 1 Kings 13:8-26, God gave a young prophet specific instruction. 1 Kings 13:8-26 (KJV)
"And the man of God said unto the king, If thou wilt give me half thine house, I will not go in with thee, neither will I eat bread nor drink water in this place: For so was it charged me by the word of the LORD, saying, Eat no bread, nor drink water, nor turn again by the same way that thou camest. So he went another way, and returned not by the way that he came to Bethel. Now there dwelt an old prophet in Bethel; and his sons came and told him all the works that the man of God had done that day in Bethel: the words which he had

spoken unto the king, them they told also to their father. And their father said unto them, What way went he? For his sons had seen what way the man of God went, which came from Judah. And he said unto his sons, Saddle me the ass. So they saddled him the ass: and he rode thereon, And went after the man of God, and found him sitting under an oak: and he said unto him, Art thou the man of God that camest from Judah? And he said, I am. Then he said unto him, Come home with me, and eat bread. And he said, I may not return with thee, nor go in with thee: neither will I eat bread nor drink water with thee in this place: For it was said to me by the word of the LORD, Thou shalt eat no bread nor drink water there, nor turn again to go by the way that thou camest. He said unto him, I am a prophet also as thou art; and an angel spake unto me by the word of the LORD, saying, Bring him back with thee into thine house, that he may eat bread and drink water. But he lied unto him. So he went back with him, and did eat bread in his house, and drank water. And it came to pass, as they sat at the table, that the word of the LORD came unto the prophet that brought him back: And he cried unto the man of God that came from Judah, saying, Thus saith the LORD, Forasmuch as thou hast disobeyed the mouth of the LORD, and hast not kept the commandment which the LORD thy God commanded thee, But camest back, and hast eaten bread and drunk water in the place, of the which the LORD did say to thee, Eat no bread, and drink no water; thy carcase shall not come unto the sepulchre of thy fathers. And it came to pass, after he had eaten bread, and after he had drunk, that he saddled for him the ass, to wit, for the prophet whom he had brought back. And when he was gone, a lion met him by the way, and slew him: and his carcase was cast in the way, and the ass stood by it, the lion also stood by the carcase. And, behold, men passed by, and saw the carcase cast in the way, *and the lion standing by the carcase: and they came and told it in the city where the old prophet dwelt. And when the prophet that brought him back from the way heard thereof, he said, It is the man of God, who was disobedient unto the word of the LORD: therefore the LORD hath delivered him unto the lion, which hath torn him, and slain him, according to the word of the LORD, which he spake unto him.*

When God gives you an instruction, do not look to people who are accustomed to disobeying God. For example, if you are a giver, your best friends should not be those who despise God's instruction when it comes to giving.

3. Show "bizdience."
Matthew 15:8 says, *"This people draw near to me with their mouth, and honor me with their lips; but their heart is far from me."*

This kind of obedience is also called eye service obedience, where you want people to see that you are doing what God asked you to do, solely for the applaud of men. Get to the point where your relationship and your obedience to God's instruction is personal, no matter who celebrates or brings you down because of it.

4. Partial obedience
An example of this kind is in the book 1st Samuel 15:18-22 *"And the Lord sent thee on a journey, and said, Go and utterly destroy the sinners the Amalekites, and fight against them until they be consumed. 19 Wherefore then didst thou not obey the voice of the Lord, but didst fly upon the spoil, and didst evil in the sight of the Lord? 20 And Saul said unto*

Samuel, Yea, I have obeyed the voice of the Lord, and have gone the way which the Lord sent me, and have brought Agag the king of Amalek, and have utterly destroyed the Amalekites. 21 But the people took of the spoil, sheep and oxen, the chief of the things which should have been utterly destroyed, to sacrifice unto the Lord thy God in Gilgal. 22 And Samuel said, Hath the Lord as great delight in burnt offerings and sacrifices, as in obeying the voice of the Lord? Behold, to obey is better than sacrifice, and to hearken than the fat of rams."

We must be careful to ensure that we are obeying God with the whole of our heart, mind, and soul; check, cross-check, and recheck.

One of the ways of enjoying the full benefit of God's supernatural dimension is to be willing and obedient, as stated in Isaiah 1:18-19,

"Come now, and let us reason together, saith the Lord: though your sins be as scarlet, they shall be as white as snow; though they be red like crimson, they shall be as wool. If ye be willing and obedient, ye shall eat the good of the land:"

When it comes to walking in obedience in order to experience the supernatural, one has got to have a renewed mindset that overshadows the natural way of thinking. After all, the spirit is always opposed to the natural man and vice versa. Hence, one must remember that to experience the supernatural via obedience, the instructions to be obeyed may not be explainable to the natural mind. For example, God told Moses to stretch forth his rod to part the sea; we read and preach about this, not thinking of the real fear that

Moses encountered at that moment. However, let's really look at it; over two million nagging people, enemies behind, and a large sea in front of them. And the best God could do was ask Moses to strike the sea. Also, how about asking the Israelites to march for six days around a city with walls 20 feet thick and then, on the 7th day, to let out a loud shout? The supernatural always comes with unnatural instructions. That's why before you decide that you really want to walk in the supernatural, you must count the cost of trusting God and be ready to look stupid to the natural man.

I remember a while back when I was struggling so much, and while at a church meeting, God instructed me to empty my account and give my money to the church. I had spent months saving this money so I could move into my new apartment and furnish it with a bed as well, and God was telling me to give it all away. Well, I trusted God, and I obeyed; it hurt because I didn't know how to get another money to get a new place, but a few months later, God provided. Another crazy instruction I received from God that permanently changed my life for good was when I got the instruction to leave my thriving Job in Nigeria (West Africa) and move to the Niger Republic to serve as a missionary with no expectation of getting paid by anyone.

I decided to resign from my Job, and all hell broke loose. My friends called me all manner of names, questioned whether or not I couldn't serve God in Nigeria; they asked me who was going to take care of my then-aging parent and why I would throw away the job that many people were looking for to go do nothing in a strange land. Interestingly, at that time, Niger Republic was one of the world's poorest countries and had a 97% Muslim population. Despite all the counsel that came from a good but natural mindset, sensible as it was, I still decided to obey God because I knew that his ways and thoughts were higher and better than mine. I arrived in Niger, and need I tell you how much of a struggle it was to survive daily; some days, I would question my decision, but I somehow held on to God's instruction. After several years, I was able to get my visa from that region to come to the United States, where I met my beautiful wife, got married, and have a family with a thriving ministry!

It takes trust and obedience to lay hands on a deformed baby in the mother's womb in prayers, believing that every deformity will be fixed. This happened to a young mother who came to me for prayers because, according to two doctor's advice, her baby was already deformed in the womb. In obedience to God, I prayed for her — asking God to correct every deformity in the baby that is still in the womb. That same month, she gave birth to a very healthy and perfect baby boy, praise God! To the natural, it's truly crazy, but obedience to the word of God is what causes the supernatural realities to become our experiences.

If you are a child of God and you are obedient to God's instructions, you will manifest the supernatural because obedience moves the hands of God.

Genesis 22:16-17, *"By myself have I sworn, saith the Lord, for because thou hast done this thing, and hast not withheld thy son, thine only son from me, I will bless thee."*

Abraham was called by God to go to a place that he had not seen or known. If for instance, I told you, "I want you to go to so-and-so place and do this and that," it will be very easy for you to obey. But if I just say, "Get in your car and start driving, and I will let you know when you get to the place," how do you know where to go? That is a vague instruction, right?

But it takes a man that trusts the instructor to take those kinds of actions. Imagine God appears to you and tells you to just get up and go to where He will show you. Think of this for a moment: now: if you were a single person, it might be easy to obey, but imagine you have a wife and kids; how do you say to your wife, "Honey, I resigned from my job; we are going somewhere that God will show us." She will definitely ask, "Honey, do you have a fever? Where are we going exactly?" "What are we going to be doing there?' you'll respond with "I don't know, but God said we should get up and go." It is crazy, right? I can't imagine the argument that can ensue from such a situation. Some good friends of yours will tell you that you are not thinking very well; how can you ask your children to leave their school and friends, and your wife to resign from her job, leave behind the business you have, and take a journey to an unknown destination?

God said, I will show you, and this man obeyed God. He obeyed God and ignored all the things that made sense to him. This man was not five years old, not even twenty years old, but seventy-five years old. That means he had established some things at this age, but he left it all behind to obey God.

There are some challenges you are facing now, and the only way to overcome them is to be obedient to an instruction that God is giving you. You may be wondering, but how can I know when God is instructing me? God gives instructions through visions, dreams, and his word. Also, God gives instruction through his servants or the pastor he has put over you. These are several ways God's instruction comes.

Your miracle lies in your obedience to God's instruction. Sometimes, we are too analytical about what God is asking us to do. We analyze the instructions that God gives to us, and the result is that we keep praying and crying when all we should have done was to be obedient for once. Many things we fast and pray for can be taken care of by a simple act of obedience. Are you ready to take your obedience to the next level?

Let Us Pray

I receive grace to obey you and honor your instructions to me even when I don't understand. I submit my intellect and emotions and I say today, not my will but yours be done, in Jesus' name. Amen!

WORKBOOK

1. What are some challenges you face in obeying God's instructions?

2. What is delayed/grumbled obedience, and how does it affect our relationship with God?

3. Reflect on a time when you struggled to trust God's instructions. What was the outcome?

4. How can we overcome these challenges and develop a renewed mindset?

5. How can you apply the principles of obedience to your life?

_____
_____
_____
_____
_____
_____
_____
_____
_____
_____
_____
_____
_____
_____
_____
_____
_____
_____
_____
_____
_____
_____
_____
_____
_____
_____
_____
_____
_____

THE REALM OF GOD — WORDS

Everything thing created is a product of words. In the realm of God, words are life, meaning they move and they perform what provoked or inspired the speaker.

Isaiah 55:11, *"So will My word be which goes out of My mouth; It will not return to Me void (useless, without result), Without accomplishing what I desire, and without succeeding in the matter for which I sent it."*

The Bible lets us know that life and death is in the power of the tongue.
Proverbs 18:21 *"The tongue has the power of life and death, and those who love it will eat its fruit."*

If we are to be in God's realm, we must also learn to speak like one who lives in that realm.
This simply means that you say what He says about your life or a situation you are going through. You are not inventing new words; you are simply declaring exactly what He has said about you. I assure you that there is no aspect of your life that God has not spoken about.
There is this temptation for us sometimes to say what

we feel when going through the storms of life. We say things like, "Allow me to express myself, it's the way I feel." But, is that how God expects you to react to what you are going through? If you want to see the supernatural, you must turn off that voice that wants you to always announce what you feel, what you hear, or what people say to you. You must get to the point where you speak like God.

Let me tell you a personal story of how my "speaking" created the life I am living now. If you have read the chapters before this, you'll be aware by now that I came from a very humble background. So humble, "the poor" called us poor. But in states of abject poverty where having the funds to travel to a nearby state in my country of origin (Nigeria) was a luxury, I always confessed that I was an American citizen. So much so that when there was a soccer match on TV, and America was playing, my friends would mockingly tell me to come to see my country (USA) playing. Everyone used to call me an American citizen until, in 2016, the words spoken over time became a reality, and I was granted citizenship. Many laughed at me then when I was making those WILD confessions; it was such a tall dream, but regardless, I called that future of mine that was not—at the time—as though it were, and now it is. The consistency of your speaking can break the spine of any situation! Your challenges may appear unbudging, but keep speaking God's words with faith, believing that God's word, which still holds the sun in the sky, is more than able to turn any situation around.

When Jesus met sick people, how did He approach them with His words? Did He not say that Lazarus and the little girl were sleeping even when all the evidence declared them dead? Would you say that Jesus was oblivious to reality, or was He being insensitive to the people's realities? What would God say if God was in need? Would God say, "I am finished; this poverty is going to drain me dead?" Is that what God would say? When Jesus was on earth, when He needed money for the taxes, He never told the disciples how they were out of cash; instead, he told them to go to the river, catch a fish, open its mouth, and get the money from its mouth. Wow, what a supernatural provision. You see, God speaks what He wants to see, not what is in front of Him.

Genesis 1:1-3, the Bible says: *"In the beginning, God created the heavens and the earth. And the earth was without form and void."*

What God was seeing was darkness upon the face of the deep. And the spirit of God was over the waters. What God was seeing was darkness. In other words, what God should have said, in our normal way, is, "Wow, I see darkness everywhere. This darkness is too thick." But God did not speak what He saw. In verse 3: *"And God said, let there be light."*

Many of us have been programmed to the "just say what you see" mindset. Some other people may interpret it as lying, but they are supernaturally ignorant. When we speak contrary to our senses, we simply switch from the natural realm to the realm of God. What happened when God said what He wanted to see in the book of Genesis? He declared light, and all

The Realm Of God—Words

of a sudden, light showed up in the midst of the darkness. I've never heard that darkness can produce light, but because God spoke, light showed up, and darkness was eliminated. God created us in his image to rule, have dominion, and reign over all His creation. Romans 4:17 "As it is written, I have made thee a father of many nations. before him whom he believed, even God, who quickened the dead, and calleth those things which be not as though they were." This simply means that you can't say I am lying because I am lacking and declaring that "I'm a rich man." If you say I'm lying, you're indirectly saying that God is encouraging lying. Because the Bible said that He called those things that He has not seen or experienced "as though they were His current realities."

When the doctor's report says that you have six months to live, God's word is saying that you will not die at a young age. So, you must choose to ignore what is practical, what is visible, and the symptoms you feel, and choose to declare what God is saying. Then, start planning for the next ten to twenty years of your life. This is how we move from the realm of the natural to operate in the realm of God.

You are a king. God says He has made you in His image,

Genesis 1:26 *"And God said: "Let us make man in our image, after our likeness, and let them have dominion over the fish of the sea, over the fowls of the air, over the cattle, and over all the earth, and over every creeping thing that crept upon the earth."*

So, God created you and gave you dominion and authority to rule. God created you as a king. Not to be

-47-

ruled over, but to rule over. When God created me, he created me with the capacity to dominate whatever space I find myself.

Every king has authority in their mouth. A king rules by decrees. If a king wants something, he speaks, and his servants and military personnel ensure that what he says becomes reality. Let's look at a scripture that paints a picture of your spiritual jurisdiction.

Proverbs 8:2 *"where the word of a king is there is power."*

In the book of Mathew 14 when Herodias' daughter danced for King Herod on his birthday, he released a word of promise from his mouth that he couldn't take back as painful as it was for him to see the fruits of it. In Matthew 14:9, it says
"Then the king regretted what he had said; but because of the vow he had made in front of his guest, he issued the necessary orders, so John was beheaded in prison."

You are not ordinary. There is power in the words you speak. And when you speak, there are spiritual entities that carry your words to ensure compliance, whether it be negative or positive.

As a pastor, whenever I speak over my congregation, I know I stand in an office to make that declaration, and their honor and expectations from the virtues in me fuel the manifestations of those things declared. I also understand that according to Isaiah 44:26, God has assured me as His called prophet;
"Establishing the words of His servant and bringing to perfection the mind of His messengers;"

I want to assure you by the word of God that you are not an ordinary entity; you are royalty whose words carry weight in the spirit realm. What differentiates the words of the ordinary person and the words of a king (you) is the power that propels the spoken word. You are not ordinary; you are a king. Revelations 1:6 states, "He has made us a kingdom of kings and priests unto our God."

Refuse to take words spoken to you lightly, even if it's a joke, the spirit realm doesn't differentiate between words spoken jokingly or seriously; words are words. No wonder Ecclesiastes 5:6 says,

"Do not let your mouth cause thy flesh to sin, and do not say before the angel that it was an error…"

When your word goes out, the enforcers carry it to ensure it comes to pass.

God honors the words of people. If you don't have this understanding, you will not know how to talk, you will not know that, from your room, you have the power to readjust your destiny, your children's lives, your community, your job, and so much more. How did prophet Elijah bring judgment to his community? It was with his words that he declared, according to the book of 1st Kings chapter 17:1

"As sure as the Lord lives, no rain or dew will fall during the next few years unless I command it."

My question to you is this: how did he "command" it? You guessed right, he commanded by speaking. Let's face it, not everyone can go out there and release words that can keep the rain from falling, but a few things make the words in your mouth powerful. You must have faith, and—by revelation—you must understand your authority in the name of Jesus, and as you declare, it must be heartfelt.

Mark 11:23 says, *"Verily, I say unto you, that whosoever shall say onto this mountain 'be thou removed and be thou cast into the sea', and shall not doubt in his heart, but shall believe that those things that he said shall come to pass, he shall have whatsoever he says."*

How many of you can pick up a 300-pound rock? As much as my kids believe that I can, I know I will end up in the ER with some sort of rupture if I attempt to lift that kind of weight. But Jesus is telling us categorically that our words can uproot a whole mountain! Think of the power it takes to destroy a mountain, the explosive power that will be used; it would take a lot of dynamite to break through a mountain. But Jesus said, the words that you speak will relocate a mountain. What Jesus is saying is that your words are greater than that explosive called dynamite; your words go with power that breaks through anything and everything.

Never trivialize what comes out of your mouth or the mouth of those around you for any reason. Through words, kings have been brought down. Through words, nations have been conquered. Through words, this earth is standing. Through words, people have died. Through words, faith is built up; through words, fear strolls in and dominates.

It was through the spoken words of the ten spies that the Israelites succumbed to fear, and God punished them for it. God affirmed what they said. Numbers 14:28

"Tell the Israelites as surely as the lord lives, I will do to them

as I have heard them say."

What is God hearing you say, what words are the angels carrying to His throne, and is the earth testifying for or against you? Yes, the Bible says even the earth hears, the rocks hear as well, anything alive has an ear, and the last time I checked, our earth is a living thing. Look at this scripture that buttresses my point.

Judges 24:27 "This stone is a witness against us, it has heard every word that God has said to us, it is a standing witness against you lest you cheat on your word."

In Jeremiah 29:29 Prophet Jeremiah was speaking to the earth *"oh earth, earth, earth, hear ye the word of the Lord…"* the earth and everything in and on it can hear the words you speak.

You must speak like God. Don't always talk out of rash emotions. Always ask yourself what you want from every situation before speaking. If you want solutions, speak solutions. Declare that it's going to be well, God is going to come through for me, this is not going to lead to death, there is testimony coming out of this." Always speak to see.

Never validate the operations of the devil in your life by confessing into your atmosphere what he is doing. When he is attacking your finances, keep declaring that "I am rich." When he is attacking your health, keep saying, "I am healed." Some people will make you feel out of place for saying what you see in the spirit as opposed to what your natural man is experiencing, and that's okay. You can't blame the blind for not seeing, and neither can you go blind to make the blind comfortable. Some will say, "We are all realistic people," in the natural world, their reality is speaking what they see, and that's okay, but in my world, my reality is speaking to see.

Never say what you don't mean. Let me put it positively: Say what you mean and mean what you say. Say what you mean and believe what you have said. (God's word) Isaiah 55:8-9 *"The words that come out of my mouth will not come back to me void but, it must accomplish the purpose for which it was sent."*

Mean every word that comes out of your mouth. Before you speak, think. Whatever you say cannot be unsaid, so say what you mean to your children and spouse, to the devil and all his attacks, and to God almighty.

When you speak, ensure that your actions align with your confession. If you are declaring healing, then by faith, get up from that sick bed and do what healed people do. The proof that you believe in your declarations is how you respond to them. We saw that when Elijah prayed for rain to return to the land, he told Ahab to get home quickly because the rain was about to fall. One day, my wife was down with a cold. She prayed over it but was still in bed under the covers, she then decided to act like a healed person so she got up from bed and went into the kitchen and started cleaning. She suddenly realized that she was healed, had no headaches or fevers, everything was gone, she felt as strong as ever. Show me your faith without works, and I will show you my faith by my works; in order words, the proof that you believe in the potency of your words is the corresponding actions after you have spoken them.

Let Us Pray
Father, help me to be like you, to be bold in my declaration despite what seems contrary. I declare that I have the grace, power, and authority to speak words that become my reality, in Jesus' name. Amen.

WORKBOOK

1. What is the relationship between words and reality, according to the text?

2. How did the author's personal experience of confessing "I am an American citizen" demonstrate the power of speaking like God?

3. What are some ways you can start exercising your authority through your words?

4. What are some examples from the Bible of people who spoke life or death through their words?

5. How did Elijah's actions demonstrate his faith in his words?

CHAPTER 5

THE REALM OF GOD — PRAYER

What is prayer? Prayer is the lifestyle of intimately communing with God to download His mind concerning any situation so His will and purpose can be enforced in your territory and every facet of your life.

Many people see prayer as a religious, mundane, and boring ritual. "Oh, if only they could understand that the world is run on prayers." Prayer is so important that Christ prescribed it to all humans in Luke 18:1

It says, "One day Jesus told his disciples a story to show that they should always pray and never give up."

Mathew 10:24-25 *"The student is not above the teacher, nor a servant above his master. It is enough for students to be like their teachers, and servants like their masters. If the head of the house has been called Beelzebul, how much more the members of his household!"*

Jesus was telling his disciples that whatever they saw in His life should be their expectations. Meaning that if He, being the son of God, prayed, then your life should also be that of prayers — there is no way around it, no substitute for prayers. Nothing moves without the fervent prayer of the righteous.

Matthew 17:21 *"Howbeit this kind goeth not out but by prayer and fasting."*

What is it that doesn't go out? These are tough situations that defy all natural and earthly help. When these moments come, be rest assured that they will come. We must tap into another realm to obtain the power sufficient enough to subdue the challenges, and the only way to tap into the supernatural (superior realm) is through prayer. Prayer is a tool for opening a portal that allows for the convergence of the natural with the supernatural realm.

Prayer is not something you do only when you feel like it. Prayer is something you must do as a Christian. Just like you don't think about your next breath, so should it be with prayers; your spirit must constantly be in communication with God.

My goal is not to get into the definition of prayer, types of prayers, and all; rather, I aim to emphasize the power of prayer, how prayer functions, and why prayer is so important. That's what we'll be looking at.

Matthew 6:5 says, *"And when you pray, do not be like the hypocrites, for they love to pray standing in the synagogues and on the street corners to be seen by others. Truly I tell you, they have received their reward in full."*

Note that Jesus said, "When you pray." He didn't say "If you pray." "If you pray" implies a probability – also, it's something that is not necessary, and you can engage in it if the occasion arises. But He said, "When you pray." "When" implies certainty — meaning that it's something expected of you to do. So, prayer is not something you should feel like doing; it's not a choice for any believer, it's not the probability of if, rather, it is the certainty of when.

I'll highlight some questions people ask all the time. If God is sovereign, omnipotent, omniscient, and omnipresent, why do we have to pray? Because when you say God is sovereign, it means God will do what He wants to do by Himself without the involvement of man. So, if God is sovereign, why pray? If God is not influenced by prayers, why should we pray? Here's another one. If God is not affected by what I do, if God will do what He wants, why pray?

Let's deal with these sincere questions. If you must begin to understand the answers to these questions, then you must first pause and ask yourself, why did Jesus pray when He was on the earth. The Bible recorded that Jesus prayed for long hours in the middle of the night. Why couldn't He just snap His fingers, and things just happened? The reason why people ask the question of "why pray?" is because they consider prayer from a selfish perspective, thinking about what they want from God.

James 4:3 *"Ye ask, and receive not, because ye ask amiss, that ye may consume it upon your lusts."*

If you look at the Lord's prayer in the book of Matthew, you'll notice it says, "thy Kingdom come, thy will be done on earth as it is in heaven" The purpose of prayer is to open the portal that grants you access to the realm of God, allowing you to see, understand, and receive His will. Through prayer, you ensure that His will is brought down to earth and carried out in your life. Prayer is the vehicle that transports spiritual realities to the earth, we are the operators of the vehicle, and the Holy Spirit is the engine. Understanding this concept will eradicate the "why pray?" question from your mind. Instead you will begin to ask, "how I can tap into the realm of God, see and understand His will, and then pray that will down to the earth."

Prayer is for alignment: When Jesus was in the garden struggling with His alignment, it was prayers that helped His flesh come into subjection to the will of God.

Matthew 26:39 *"He went on a little farther and bowed with his face to the ground, praying, "My Father! If it is possible, let this cup of suffering be taken away from me. Yet I want your will to be done, not mine."*

Prayer is for communion and intercourse with God to be transformed into His likeness and His image. Can you imagine married couples relating with each other simply because they want something from one another? That would be a transactional relationship, and at some point, both parties would feel used. Prayer is not just about what you want; it is about fellowship that produces intimacy, and that is what it is about.

Prayer is also a way to acknowledge your inadequacies and admitting your needs and desires to God. So, why pray? Because the Bible says whatsoever you need, "when you pray," it will be met according to His riches in Christ Jesus. We already understand that our prayers create channels through which our needs can be met; it is a requirement, and it is the kingdom protocol, the modus operandi of the kingdom.

Matthew 7:7 *"Ask and you shall receive."*

The sovereignty of God does not negate your responsibility to pray. God's sovereignty is limited to His word. When you are going on a journey, and there is a bridge with guard rail on both sides of it, everything you do will have to be between the guard rail if you must be safe. So, when God spoke, He confined himself to the guard rails of His word. God will not do anything out of His word. In other words, God's limitation is based on what He has said. He said in the book of Isaiah 55:11,
"My word will not come back to me void, but it must accomplish the purpose for which it was spoken."

Also, Psalms 139:2 says, *"I worship towards thy holy temple and praise thy name for thy loving kindness and for thy truth, for thou has magnified thy word above your names."*

God has commanded you in His infallible word to pray to receive so if you don't pray, you do so at your own risk.
Some people in their bid to cajole God to do what they want, will say "If you are God, you have to do this," even when the thing is contrary to God's word. God will not compromise His integrity to prove to you that

He is God. So, if you are praying outside God's will, and making declarations, calling God by all His names, God will not budge! For your prayers to have any spiritual impact, you must ensure that they are aligned with His words.

WHY IT IS IMPORTANT TO PRAY

God gave man dominion over the earth. The reason we pray is for heaven to intervene on earth and for the sovereignty of God to be manifested in our daily lives. Letting the kingdom of God come on the earth is not a thing that will happen by chance; God will not impose Himself on the earth; He must be called upon by human agencies.

Genesis 1:26. *"And God said, let us make man in our image, after our likeness, and let them have dominion over the fish of the sea, and over the fowls of the air, and over the cattle, and over all the earth."*

God's desire is to make an extension of Himself that will be called man, a representative that controls the earth while He controls the heavens. We are stewards of the earth. Have you ever wondered why God didn't question Adam's decisions as he named all the animals? Is it written in any part of the scriptures that as Adam named the animals, this is a lion, an elephant, a tiger, a gorilla, that God interrupted, saying, "Adam, you can't call this a tiger. That should be a chimpanzee." God did not question Adam's authority because He gave it to him so he could properly dominate the earth and all within it. Take note of this because this will change the dynamics of your prayer. It will make you see prayer as something that must happen instead of a mere religious activity.

Psalm 115:16 *"The heavens of the heavens belong to God, but the earth he has given to man."*

Let me use one of my businesses to explain to you what I mean by "God gave us dominion over the earth." I have several independent living facilities, and I gave authority to those I made supervisors over those homes. When some residents call me to complain about something, I ask, "Have you spoken with the supervisor?" I gave him authority and jurisdiction to respond to numerous problems that may occur with the residence so he handles issues on my behalf. Often there is usually no need for me to be present there because my representative makes the same decision that I would have taken based on the house rules.

For God to intervene in earthly matters, someone who has the legal right to be here on the earth (man) has to invite Him, and the invitation is sent to God through prayers.

God was desperate to rescue humanity from the bondage of sin but had to do so within His protocol, so as humbling as it was, Jesus had to become human, to have flesh and blood, so He came through the doorway — called the human birth.

So, Jesus had legal authority to operate here on earth. While He was on the earth, He prayed always because He had put on humanity, He was now also a man, and Luke 18:1 emphasizes that *"men ought always to pray."*

He came to the earth to have legal authority, to permit

or to give license to His supernatural being to manifest and put the works of the devil to an end. Because of His consistent prayers, people began to see the supernatural hand of God. The blind received their sight, the lame walked, and even the dead came back to life!

The disciples were in awe of His operations, but they were sensible enough that they didn't ask Him to teach them how to perform miracles or how to command the people's attention with great preaching. They understood that something was empowering Him to do unusual things, and they asked Him to help them with that. They said, "Master, teach us to pray."

There are so many instances in the scriptures where if had God not been invited; it would have turned out terribly. Let's look at the scenario in the scriptures that pertains to two men of the same faith in the same situation.

Acts 12:1-6 *(KJV)*

Now about that time Herod the king stretched forth his hands to vex certain of the church. And he killed James the brother of John with the sword. And because he saw it pleased the Jews, he proceeded further to take Peter also. (Then were the days of unleavened bread.) And when he had apprehended him, he put him in prison, and delivered him to four quaternions of soldiers to keep him; intending after Easter to bring him forth to the people. Peter therefore was kept in prison: but prayer was made without ceasing of the church unto God for him. And when Herod would have brought him forth, the same night Peter was sleeping between two soldiers, bound with two chains: and the keepers before the door kept the prison.

These two men of God were in the same situation. *But why* did one die? Was God partial? Did he prefer Peter to James? Was the angel that delivered Peter on an errand when James was executed? The difference between James and Peter's outcome is the prayers that went up. After James had died, the disciples realized that "God is not going to come down unless we call on Him." So, the Bible says that they prayed continuously until help came. God was not partial, it's just that the protocol for supernatural intervention was not obeyed. The protocol is that we pray. When we pray, we permit God to intervene with the supernatural and throw all our inadequacies on Him. The Bible says, "My spirit will not strive with man anymore." No matter how bad your situation is, if you keep crying, wailing, lamenting, and talking to your situation without getting God involved, God will be where He is. He has already let you know that all you have to do is call His name. The Bible says that "Whoever shall call upon the name of the Lord shall be saved." So, if you are not calling upon His name, you are not permitting him. He is a gentle entity. He will not barge into your life. He will come when invited. And prayer is the sure way to get help from God.

Some years ago, my family was going through very tough financial times, I did everything I could, had various interviews for a particular job, and got rejected every time — in a nutshell, we really struggled. Now, being that I was of God, why didn't He do anything about it? But the Bible says, "My people perish for lack of knowledge." So, I went into seclusion for some heartfelt prayers. After my intense and focused prayer, that same week, I had a vision where God assured me of my victory. The same job I applied for and was getting rejected — interview upon interview, I did the same interviews again and got two jobs both paying me six figures. If I hadn't prayed, nothing would have moved in the spirit realm.

Ezekiel 22:30 *"And I sought for a man among them that should make up the hedge and stand in the gap before Me for the land, that I should not destroy it; but I found none."*

2 Chronicles 14:14 says, *"If my people, which are called by my name, shall humble themselves, and pray, and seek my face, and turn from their wicked ways; then will I hear from heaven, and will forgive their sin, and will heal their land."*

All these wonderful things will happen but only at the instance of prayers.

Prayer is the greatest force we have.
It forces things in and out of place. A prophet came to a man and told him to put his house in order because his death was imminent. But this man, Hezekiah, turned his face to the wall and prayed his way out of death.

Isaiah 38:1-6 says, *"Isaiah 38:1-6 (KJV)*
In those days was Hezekiah sick unto death. And Isaiah the prophet the son of Amoz came unto him, and said unto him, Thus saith the LORD, Set thine house in order: for thou shalt die, and not live. Then Hezekiah turned his face toward the wall, and prayed unto the LORD, And said, Remember now, O LORD, I beseech thee, how I have walked before thee in truth and with a perfect heart, and have done that which is

good in thy sight. And Hezekiah wept sore. Then came the word of the LORD to Isaiah, saying, Go, and say to Hezekiah, Thus saith the LORD, the God of David thy father, I have heard thy prayer, I have seen thy tears: behold, I will add unto thy days fifteen years. And I will deliver thee and this city out of the hand of the king of Assyria: and I will defend this city."

When Hezekiah heard this, he turned his face to the wall and prayed to the Lord, "Remember, O Lord, how I have always been faithful to you and have served you single-mindedly, always doing what pleases you." Then he broke down and wept bitterly.

Then this message came to Isaiah from the Lord: "Go back to Hezekiah and tell him, 'This is what the Lord, the God of your ancestor David, says: I have heard your prayer and seen your tears. I will add fifteen years to your life, and I will rescue you and this city from the king of Assyria. Yes, I will defend this city."

There was a time when we had no money to pay our church rent, but we had to keep on praying and believing. One Sunday morning, I was preaching so passionately about faith and what God can do, and the devil was telling me that I would be put to shame because the church would be kicked out of the building. While I preached, my heart pounded, but I still held on to my faith in God. After the message, we too our offering, and a guest put a fat envelope in the offering basket. In my mind, I assumed that it was going to be one dollar bill; in my life, I had learned not to put my trust in men — when I got the financial report, I was told that the offering of that particular guest was

$1400. That was more than enough to pay the rent for that month, in my mind, I began to think that this person will be the financier of the ministry, but that was the last time he ever gave that kind of offering again. Our prayer forced this man out of wherever he was to come and drop that offering in our ministry. Indeed, James 5:16 couldn't say it any better, *"The earnest prayer of a righteous person has great power and produces wonderful results."*

We prayed fervently and believed wholeheartedly, and God came through.

One more testimony that shows the forceful power of prayer to move things for you happened in 2012.

My apartment rent was overdue, and we had already been given an eviction notice; I tried everything I could at the time to get the rent. Back then, I used to flip cars; I would buy a car, fix it up mildly, and sell it as it is. My entire hope rested on selling the car and using the proceeds to pay the rent, but that door seemed jammed. Several people came by to look at the car, but no one bought it. I was getting frustrated; no one had any money to lend me at that time as well.

I was now thinking how my family would be homeless; needless to say, I prayed earnestly through this process for God to show up, and must I say that the money came from the most unexpected place. From a friend of mine from Nigeria, this was so unexpected because those of us (Nigerians) who have left the shores of our home country are usually the ones to send money back home because there exists a perception that we are in greener pastures. Still on this testimony, my friend called me one morning while I was just thinking of how to get the rent paid, not just that, but the extra fees for paying late. He said he was in his church back home and was about to pay his tithe but God laid in his heart to send it to me. My jaw dropped! God showed up indeed from the most unlikely place. God yet again used our prayers to move someone's heart to answer our prayers.

Prayer is for influence:
Before I embark on any venture or have to meet with someone, I need a favor from, I sit on it first in prayers. I call on God to touch and turn the person's heart to favor me. I pray for alignment of my words with their heart, and God always comes through. Let me share this testimony with you: I came to the United States with a visiting visa. While I was in the country, a ministry wanted me to work with them, but I was almost running out of status and had to renew my visa to be in status before I filled for a religious visa. However, the timing to apply for a religious visa was out of place because I had only two weeks left on my visa. The required amount of time needed to even attempt to apply for an extension of my visiting visa was between 30-45 days. This situation didn't bother me because I knew that when I prayed, God would move. I prayerfully applied and prayerfully waited; in my prayers, I committed the United States Citizens and Immigration Services (USCIS) into God's hands. I prayed specifically for the person who was going to be handling my file that they would favor me. God showed up; I was granted the extension despite the

odds surrounding my application. In continuation to this testimony, after I had received my extension, it was now time to apply for a religious visa. So, myself and the senior pastor I was working with went to see an immigration lawyer. I was told that after the tragic 9-11 incident, they had limited the number of religious visas issued; even if they issued any, it would be one out of every hundred applicants. Also, the lawyer said he would try, but the price was outrageous, and there was no guarantee that it would be granted. The senior pastor and I agreed in prayers that the same God who approved the extension was would do this one. So, we filled it ourselves without going through the lawyer and, again, prayerfully waited. I am sure you know how this story ends: God showed up again, I had favor with the USCIS, my religious visa was approved, and it was possible because we prayed.

I share this story to let you know that with prayers, we can influence decisions to favor us, influence policies, and change the minds of kings!

Prayer fosters intimacy

Prayer shouldn't be engaged only when you need something. There are some people you relate with to the extent that even when you don't see them, you are familiar with their voice because of frequent communication. I remember there was a time when I changed my phone, some of my contacts called me, and I couldn't recognize their voices. However, when those I often communicate with called, I instantly recognized their voices. Talk to God often and go into prayers just to thank Him for what He has already done. Say prayers of worship, of desire to know Him and hear His voice, and to love on Him in prayers. He will make Himself known to you, and you will be known by Him.

How many of you are ready to bring the supernatural to the natural? Going forward, anytime you hear "let us pray," see it as an opportunity to cause heaven to invade the earth.

Let Us Pray.

Lord, help me cultivate a habit of prayer; let the spirit of prayer and supplication rest on me. I know that I am in partnership with you to enforce your will on the earth. I am a man/woman of effective prayers in Jesus' name. Amen.

WORKBOOK

1. What is prayer, according to the text?

2. How does Psalm 115:16 highlight humanity's role in praying for God's intervention?

3. How did Hezekiah's prayer in Isaiah 38:1-6 demonstrate the power of prayer?

4. How can prayer foster intimacy with God?

5. How can you apply the principles of prayer to your life?

_____

_____

_____

_____

_____

_____

_____

_____

_____

_____

_____

_____

_____

_____

_____

_____

_____

_____

_____

_____

_____

_____

_____

_____

_____

_____

_____

_____

_____

CHAPTER 6

THE REALM OF GOD—FAITH

I f you desire to see the supernatural move of God, then you have no choice but to believe because it takes faith to tap into the supernatural world. So then, what is faith? It simply means accepting the word of God and acting on it. It's not enough to accept and believe it, but acting on the word is proof of faith.

Faith is taking sides with the word of God, against the words and the operations of the enemy. Faith is belief in God beyond what you see and acting according to what you say you believe.

There is no transaction between the natural and the supernatural realm without faith. If you go through the Bible, from Genesis to Revelation, you'll observe that God will always bring a man to the point of believing in Him before any action or manifestation of the supernatural can be carried out. God went all the way with Gideon when the angel that appeared to him had to perform all manner of miracles for Gideon to believe in the message the angel delivered.

Judges 6:36-40, *"So Gideon said to God, "If You will save Israel by my hand as You have said — look, I shall put a fleece of wool on the threshing floor; if there is dew on the fleece only, and it is dry on all the ground, then I shall know that You will save Israel by my hand, as You have said." And it was so. When he rose early the next morning and squeezed the fleece together, he wrung the dew out of the fleece, a bowlful of water. Then Gideon said to God, "Do not be angry with me, but let me speak just once more: Let me test, I pray, just once more with the fleece; let it now be dry only on the fleece, but on all the ground let there be dew." And God did so that night. It was dry on the fleece only, but there was dew on all the ground."*

God did this for Gideon not as a magical treat but to establish faith in him. This does not mean that in all your interactions with God, you must ask for a sign; remember what faith is, "evidence of things not seen." The Bible makes us understand that blessed is he who has not seen but believes. When one of Jesus' disciples, Thomas was told that Jesus had risen from the dead, he wanted proof before he believed. Jesus did give him the proof he needed but also admonished him to believe before seeing.

Jesus often times asked those who were seeking to be healed if they believed before he healed them.

Matthew 9:28, *"And Jesus said to them, "Do you believe that I am able to do this?" They said to Him, "Yes, Lord." Then He touched their eyes, saying, "According to your faith let it be to you." And their eyes were opened."*

There is a special breed of people that live the way God approves of — "The just."

Romans 1:17 *"Therein is the righteousness of God revealed from faith to faith, as it is written, "For the just shall live by faith."*

The just will not live by their bank account; they shall not live by the medications they take—"the, just" shall live by faith. Therefore, there is no release from heaven without something coming from you that provokes that heavenly blessing, and that is faith. Faith is the currency by which transactions are made from the supernatural to the natural world.

The reason why we see less of God's hands in our world today is simple. We have gotten to a point where we just trust our senses, science, technologies, and experiences more than we trust the word of God. We have become too rational, too realistic, and too "intelligent" to tap into the faith realm. What we can physically experience with our senses is what forms our thoughts and actions. But God is looking for men and women who will trust Him beyond what the doctor's report is saying, beyond the policy of the government, and more than what the financial analysts is saying.

When they say that there's going to be a recession, your faith is saying, "God will supply all my needs according to His riches in glory." God is looking for men who will force that word into reality by their faith.

I remember when I was about to get married, I wasn't really doing much then, and finance was a big issue; I had already set the wedding date with my now wife by faith and did not want to default or change my mind. I remember many people asking me how I was going to get married without a working system for finances. However, I was ready to get married regardless because I was already in my mid-thirties, and I wasn't going to wait for all the stars to align. I was going to let God be my Father and sponsor my wedding. I'm not sure how many more years I would have waited if I had to save up the money, considering the fact that I was almost at minimum wage and my wife was not doing much as she had just arrived in the country and was still trying to get her feet wet. She was an orphan, so she had no one to sponsor her; it was either God who showed up or God showed up. Someone came up to me to ask if I had a plan B, or I was only relying on faith for this wedding. My response to that person was this, "If I have a Plan B, where then is my faith?"

Other people told me to postpone the wedding till I had the money to do it, but I was not planning this wedding based on my pocket but on heaven's bank. My faith was radical, I was desperate to see and know that truly God responds to those who are crazy enough to believe Him for the impossible. A few days before the wedding, a lot of things were still not done: we had no wedding ring, I had no bed in my one-bedroom apartment, and my fiancée was beginning to get worried.

So, I called and told her to remove her mind from the process of the wedding and just picture us on the wedding night, kneeling in our apartment and thanking God for His supernatural provision. About two to three days before the wedding, God supernaturally provided everything we needed.

I was able to get the rings and the hall paid for, and of course, God provided enough for me to get a bed in my bedroom so my new bride wouldn't sleep on the floor on her wedding night. Truth be told, I can't really explain how all the finances came about, but I know that God started working on my behalf and touching the hearts of men for my sake. The wedding was a great success, and there was no debt owed during the whole process!

God is pleased when we give Him a good challenge. Many people think they have faith, but in actual sense, they just have a plan B, or they believe in something that anyone can do for them. To really put your faith to the test would be that moment when your ONLY option is God!

Hebrew 11:6 says: *"But without faith, it is impossible to please God." It does not say 'Without faith it is hard to please God.' If it is hard, it means that there's a possibility that you can please God without faith. But it says that without faith, it is impossible to please God. It says: "For he that cometh to God must believe that he is the rewarder of them that diligently seek him."*

If it is impossible to please God without faith, then getting something from Him whom you can't please is also impossible.

This truth is evident in Jesus' ministry, the one who came from heaven with all kinds of power — 100% man and God. While Jesus was on earth performing all manner of miracles everywhere He went, unfortunately, He couldn't do much in the city He came from. The unbelieving town, Nazareth missed every divine intervention required for the manifestations of their destinies because of their lack of faith. Their familiarity with Jesus sponsored their disbelief in Him. So, although Jesus, being full of compassion, tried to heal them, He could not because perhaps while He was laying hands on them, they were staring at Him in the face, not with awe-filled expectation but with that sense of familiarity. Many of them just went to Him to see if what they've been hearing was true, with no single faith attached to their actions toward Him. What a missed opportunity; how sad. Matthew 13:58 *"And he did not do many miracles there because of their lack of faith."*

The reason why we don't receive as much as we should is because we have been so mentally programmed to believe that the only way to succeed is that one plus one has to be two. If this is not the case, we don't stretch our minds beyond the possibilities of the five senses. God is saying it doesn't have to be this way. Let's look at

Matthew 8:26: *"He said unto them: Why are ye fearful, oh ye of little faith." Then, he arose and rebuked the winds and the sea, and there was a great calm." The disciples of Jesus were with Jesus in the sea, in the boat, and there was a great storm. They forgot that the messiah was with them, they were shouting and crying. They said to Jesus, "Master, are you sleeping? don't you know we are going to perish?"*

After Jesus rebuked the storm, He then turned around and rebuked them for their lack of faith.
"Don't you know that the king of kings resides within you in this boat called life? Don't you know that the God of heaven is living inside of you? God is asking,

how is it that you trust your circumstances more than you trust me? Oh, ye of little faith."

Did you know that the disciples would have been able to rebuke the storm without Jesus's intervention? I know this based on Jesus' response to their cry for help. Jesus was telling them that they would have been able to do it. He did not say, "I don't blame your little faith; you have not gotten to that point yet." He didn't say, "It's because you've not prayed enough." Instead, He said, "Ye men of little faith," meaning that if they had faith, the miracle would have happened. If one of them had dared to stand up against the storm and said, "In the name of Jesus, I command you to be still," maybe that would have been the first time they would have recorded a disciple performing a miracle.

Well, no one dared to do it. Some of you stand before your situations and your problems, and you begin to cry, panic, and worry. You wail out, "Oh my God, why is this happening to me?" How many of you have ever blamed the children of Israel for all their faithlessness? God does something miraculous in their time of need but after a while, when they see another trouble, they start shouting, "Oh no, we have to return to Egypt; this problem will kill us." We all react this way sometimes, don't we? Can you ponder how many circumstances God has delivered you from? However, when the next challenge raises its ugly head, you go on and panic as if you are unaware of the power of God. Count your blessings one by one, and see what God has done for you as a testament that He will always come through for you.

One of my favorite people in scripture is Caleb; he had

this consistent faith that carried on until he was old. Let us look at Caleb's faith at forty-five years and his faith at eight-five years.

Numbers 14:1-9 *"And all the congregation lifted up their voice, and cried; and the people wept that night. And all the children of Israel murmured against Moses and against Aaron: and the whole congregation said unto them, Would God that we had died in the land of Egypt! or would God we had died in this wilderness! And wherefore hath the LORD brought us unto this land, to fall by the sword, that our wives and our children should be a prey? were it not better for us to return into Egypt? And they said one to another, Let us make a captain, and let us return into Egypt. Then Moses and Aaron fell on their faces before all the assembly of the congregation of the children of Israel. And Joshua the son of Nun, and Caleb the son of Jephunneh, which were of them that searched the land, rent their clothes: And they spake unto all the company of the children of Israel, saying, The land, which we passed through to search it, is an exceeding good land. If the LORD delight in us, then he will bring us into this land, and give it us; a land which floweth with milk and honey. Only rebel not ye against the LORD, neither fear ye the people of the land; for they are bread for us: their defence is departed from them, and the LORD is with us: fear them not. "*

Joshua 14:10-12

"Now then, just as the Lord promised, he has kept me alive for forty-five years since the time he said this to Moses, while Israel moved about in the wilderness. So here I am today, eighty-five years old! I am still as strong today as the day Moses sent me out; I'm just as vigorous to go out to battle

now as I was then. Now give me this hill country that the Lord promised me that day. You yourself heard then that the Anakites were there, and their cities were large and fortified, but the Lord helping me, I will drive them out just as he said."

At this point, Caleb was eighty-five years old. The same faith he had when he and the other eleven spied on the land of Canaan is the same faith he had when he was old and desired another land.

God didn't create us to live by our natural feelings alone. Scriptures upon scriptures, Old and New Testament emphasize that we must live by faith. Repetition of a thing usually depicts the importance of it.

Romans 1:17, *For in it the righteousness of God is revealed from faith to faith; as it is written, "The just shall live by faith."*

Galatians 3:11, *But that no one is justified by the law in the sight of God is evident, for "the just shall live by faith.*

Hebrews 10:38, *"Now the just shall live by faith but if anyone draws back, my soul has no pleasure in him."*

Habakkuk 2:4, *"Behold the proud, his soul is not upright in him; But the just shall live by his faith.*

Mark 11:23, *The Bible says: "For verily I say unto you, that whosoever shall say unto this mountain 'be thou removed and be thy cast into the sea', and shall not doubt in his heart, but shall believe that those things that he says shall come to pass, he shall have whatsoever he saith." Emphasis on the words 'shall not doubt but shall believe.'*

Declare, speak over your life — that there shall be great manifestations of God's presence; that although a thousand shall fall at your side, you shall not be moved. You may have a diagnosis that has killed other people — but you declare that this is not unto death — the hand of the Lord will save you from this circumstance. You will see whatever you say if you don't doubt.

All who received the miracles or experienced the supernatural move of God in the ministry of Jesus Christ did so by faith. Let's look at the woman with the issue of blood. Do you know that many people with health issues were close to Jesus but did not get healed? Let's look at

Mark 5:34, *"And he said unto her, 'Daughter, thy faith hath made thee whole. Go in peace and be whole of thy plague." He didn't say, "Woman, my power has healed you." He didn't say, "Woman, the environment you are in, has brought the miracle." He said, "Your faith."*

No wonder thousands of people can be in a church, and prayers will be made, but a few of the congregants come up to testify of the miracle they received as a result of the prayers, yet some don't testify. They go back with their problems, claiming that those who testified lied or that God doesn't love them enough to have healed them as well. That mindset alone is full of disbelief and won't receive anything from God.

Hebrews 4:2 says, *"For indeed we have had the glad tidings [Gospel of God] proclaimed to us just as truly as they [the*

Israelites of old did when the good news of deliverance from bondage came to them]; but the message they heard did not benefit them, because it was not mixed with faith (with the leaning of the entire personality on God in absolute trust and confidence in His power, wisdom, and goodness) by those who heard it; neither were they united in faith with the ones [Joshua and Caleb] who heard (did believe)"

This means that whatever happens to you when God's word comes depends on you. Your faith is what takes a logos word and transforms it into a rhema word. Faith comes by hearing the word, but the power in that word is activated and released through faith.

You either only believe in the word, or you can believe and act on the word. James said, "Show me your faith without works, and I will show you my faith by my works." If you say you will be healed but still talk about the sickness to everyone who cares to ask, you are in denial of faith and can't be healed. Also, if you say you will have children, have you named your unborn kids, have you bought their clothes and prepared their rooms? Real faith makes you look stupid to those who only know of the earthly realm. Spirits and humans have different possibilities, as well as the supernatural and natural realms, but the supernatural realm is superior. One plus one equals two in the natural realm, but in the spiritual realm, it could equal 500.

Truth is, you cannot see supernatural things when you are still operating with logic (the 1+1=2 mentality). You can only experience the supernatural when you have one plus one and you are expecting more than two.

Another moment I want to look at in the ministry of

Jesus is in Matthew 9:28-29. The Bible says:
"And when he was come into the house, the blind man Came to him and Jesus said unto them, 'Believe ye that I am able to do this." And all of them, unanimously, said unto him, 'yes, Lord, we believe. Amen. Hallelujah. *Verse 29. "He touched their eyes, saying 'according to your faith."*

Did you see that? If God said to you today, According to your faith," how many of you will receive your miracles?

The centurion servant that came to Jesus Christ exercised a kind of faith that Jesus appreciated. Jesus Christ compared him with the Israelites. He said, "I have never seen any man in Israel that has this kind of faith."

Jesus said, "I want to come and heal your servant." The man says, "Master, I am a man with authority. When I speak to people that are under me to do this, they do it. Just speak the word." He had faith in the words that Jesus would speak to him. SELAH!

A FEW THINGS TO TAKE NOTE OF ABOUT FAITH
1. Your faith must be based on God's word.
Romans 10:17, *"Faith comes by hearing and hearing by the word of God." You can't have faith that is contrary to God's word. Whatever you are praying for, always look for the scriptural backing for it. Where in the scripture did God promise you what you are having faith for?*

That is why when we pray with the word of God, we pray in the will of God. The Bible says that many people pray, and they don't receive because they pray amiss; they are asking things out of God's will. So, if you must have faith, it has to be within the parameters of God's will. If you are sick and the doctor says it is a terminal disease, you can trust God that His word says that your days shall be one hundred and twenty years on earth. God will answer that prayer because it is word-based.

2 Faith is not denying the obvious facts but trusting God's word and power over and above it all.

Your faith insists that you are coming out of every unpleasant situation despite all the odds stacked up against your hopes.

John 11:23-27. "*Jesus saith unto her, Thy brother shall rise again. Martha saith unto him, I know that he shall rise again in the resurrection at the last day. Jesus said unto her, I am the resurrection, and the life: he that believeth in me, though he were dead, yet shall he live: And whosoever liveth and believeth in me shall never die. Believest thou this? She saith unto him, Yea, Lord: I believe that thou art the Christ, the Son of God, which should come into the world.*"

3. When acting in faith, physical evidence is not needed or necessary.

Some of us only want to trust God — for the things that we can see — which are possible in the lives of others. You don't need prior evidence to know that God can do something. Child of God, stay away from trying to know if this will happen first before you have faith. Some people want to hear that it has happened before, that God has done it before in the life of another before they have faith. God can start it with you. Some of the things we read in the Bible happened to the people first, and it was recorded, and that is why we say God can do it. For instance, Moses was the first to part the Red Sea, etc. The weather can be dark, and you believe there's going to be sunshine; you may not see any sign of the sun, but you trust God despite the impossibilities; if you stand on your word-based faith, God will respond to it, causing the sun to shine amid the darkness. Based on scriptures, there had not been any prior miracle of the sun standing still for Joshua to have referenced or based his faith on but he stood and declared by faith, "Let the sun stand still," and it did!

Hebrews 11:1 says, *"Now faith is the substance of things hoped for, the evidence of things not seen."*

Joshua did not need any physical or historical evidence; Faith alone was his evidence.
Let's begin to trust God for the supernatural, the realm where all things are possible. What is it that you want to do that has not been done in your family before? You can trust God for that.

Let Us Pray
Father, I confess all my unbelief to you; I chose to take you at your word no matter what seems to contradict it. I receive the grace and strength already made available for me to become all you intend for me to become in Jesus' name. Amen.

WORKBOOK

1. What is faith, according to the text?

2. How did Gideon demonstrate his faith in God?

3. How does faith relate to the natural and supernatural realms?

4. How can you overcome unbelief and trust God's word?

5. What is one area of your life where you need to apply faith?

_____
_____
_____
_____
_____
_____
_____
_____
_____
_____
_____
_____
_____
_____
_____
_____
_____
_____
_____
_____
_____
_____
_____
_____
_____
_____
_____
_____
_____
_____
_____

_____
_____
_____
_____
_____
_____
_____
_____
_____
_____
_____
_____
_____
_____
_____
_____
_____
_____
_____
_____
_____
_____
_____
_____
_____
_____
_____
_____
_____
_____

CONCLUSION

I want to encourage you to tap into your greatness in all that God has provided for us in Christ Jesus.
Everything you need to access realm of God is already at your disposal.

2 Peter 1:3 says, *"His divine power hath given unto us all things that pertain unto life and godliness, through the knowledge of Him that hath called us to glory and virtue."*
The earth, creation itself, is anxiously waiting for us to rise into our responsibilities.

Romans 8:19-22 says, *"For the earnest expectation of the creature waiteth for the manifestation of the sons of God.*
For the creature was made subject to vanity, not willingly, but by reason of him who hath subjected the same in hope, Because the creature itself also shall be delivered from the bondage of corruption into the glorious liberty of the children of God. For we know that the whole creation groaneth and travaileth in pain together until now."

We cannot make any meaningful impact that will cause the world to stop and listen to us if everything we do is basic and natural. As much as it looks like many people keep rejecting Christ, they really don't want to. This is because we only present to them the one-dimensional part of the gospel; the gospel is not just in words but also power.
To access the power that is already within us requires drilling our spirit man, a pressing of the olive to release the oil. The power already within us will not be manifested if we are unaware of our dire need for it. If

we are nonchalant about God's desire for our awareness of it, working back-to-back to pay bills and ignoring the power within us to make real wealth, and sitting and scrolling on our phones for hours, we can never activate that power. The power to tap into the supernatural will only be activated through digging the wells of our spirit in prayers, fasting, deep meditations on the word, and going out to prove the word in practice.

Enough of the world laughing at us, enough of settling for a power-deficient life; let's show the world whose God is God; let's make them see that all we talk about in the Bible is true and real and can be experienced today.

Are you ready to dust off yourself and join me on this journey of functioning from the realm of God?

I will leave you with this creed that we share in my church. Meditate on each line and keep declaring it.

"We are citizens of the kingdom, we live by the word of God, we have a divine nature, we have dominion over our world."